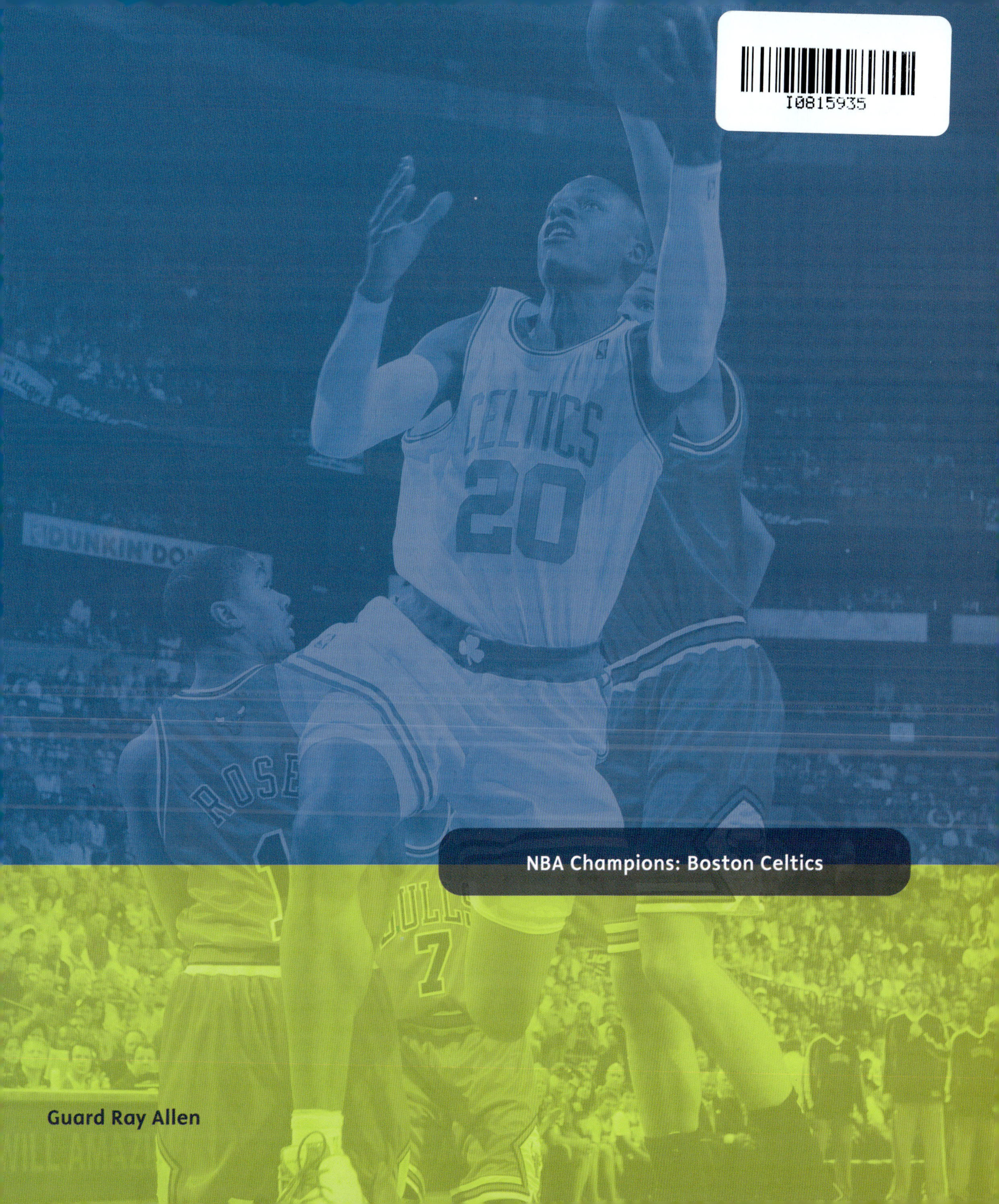

Guard Ray Allen

Point guard Dee Brown

NBA CHAMPIONS

# BOSTON CELTICS

JOE TISCHLER

CREATIVE EDUCATION / CREATIVE PAPERBACKS

**Power forward Kevin Garnett**

Published by Creative Education and Creative Paperbacks
P.O. Box 227, Mankato, Minnesota 56002
Creative Education and Creative Paperbacks are imprints of
The Creative Company
www.thecreativecompany.us

Art Direction by Tom Morgan
Book production by Graham Morgan
Edited by Grace Cain

Images by Getty Images/Alex Bierens de Haan, 10, Andrew D. Bernstein, cover, 16, Brian Babineau, 1, 4, 7, Carmen Mandato, cover, Dick Raphael, 15, 19, Gregory Shamus, 20, Manny Millan, 6, Mitchell Leff, 3, Nathaniel S. Butler, 2, NBA Photos, 5, Steve Babineau, 12, Steve Dunwell, 9, Steven Ryan, 24



Library of Congress Cataloging-in-Publication Data

Names: Tischler, Joe, author.
Title: Boston Celtics / Joe Tischler.
Description: Mankato, Minnesota : Creative Education and Creative Paperbacks, [2025] | Series: Creative sports: nba champions | Includes index. | Audience: Ages 7-10 | Audience: Grades 2-3 | Summary: "Elementary-level text and dynamic sports photos highlight the NBA championship wins of the Boston Celtics, plus sensational players associated with the professional basketball team such as Jayson Tatum"—Provided by publisher.
Identifiers: LCCN 2024014044 (print) | LCCN 2024014045 (ebook) | ISBN 9798889892502 (library binding) | ISBN 9781682776162 (paperback) | ISBN 9798889893615 (ebook)
Subjects: LCSH: Boston Celtics (Basketball team)—History—Juvenile literature. | Basketball players—United States—Juvenile literature.
Classification: LCC GV885.52.B67 T57 2025 (print) | LCC GV885.52.B67 (ebook) | DDC 796.323/640974461—dc23/eng/20240404
LC record available at https://lccn.loc.gov/2024014044
LC ebook record available at https://lccn.loc.gov/2024014045

Printed in China

Center Robert Parish

Small forward John Havlicek

CONTENTS

# Home of the Celtics

Boston, Massachusetts is a city rich in history. It is well known for Paul Revere's midnight ride. It is also known for the Boston Tea Party. A basketball team rich in history plays there, too. It's the Celtics. They play their home games at TD Garden.

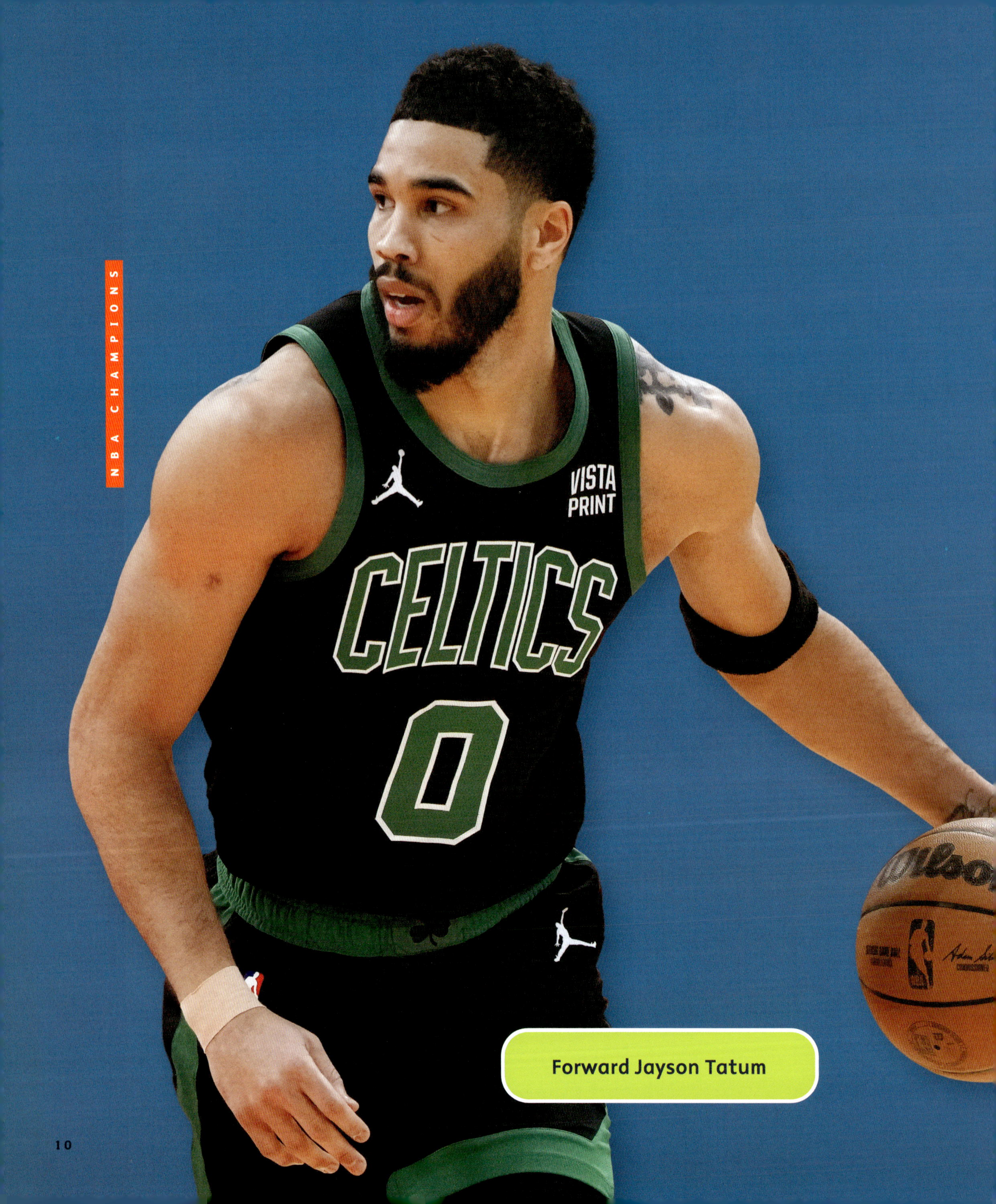

Forward Jayson Tatum

he Boston Celtics are a National Basketball Association (NBA) team. They play in the Atlantic Division. That's part of the Eastern Conference. Their **rivals** are the Philadelphia 76ers and Los Angeles Lakers. All NBA teams want to win the NBA Finals and become champions. The Celtics have won a record 18 championships!

Small forward Paul Pierce

# Naming the Celtics

The team's first owner picked the team name. Boston has a large Irish population. People from Ireland are often called "Celtics." The original owner of the team was also fond of the Original Celtics. They were a **barnstorming** team from the 1920s.

# Celtics History

The Celtics began to play in 1946. They were one of the original teams of the NBA. Bill Russell was one of the team's first stars. He arrived in Boston for the 1956–57 season. The Celtics won their first **title** that year. He played 12 more years in Boston. The Celtics won 10 more championships during that time. Russell was named NBA **Most Valuable Player (MVP)** five times.

From 1959–69, the Celtics played the Los Angeles Lakers seven times in the NBA Finals. Boston won each time. Bob Cousy was on most of

Point guard Jo Jo White

Power forward Larry Bird

those teams. He was great at giving **assists**. Sam Jones was great at scoring.

The Celtics kept on winning titles. They won in 1974. And again in 1976. Star forward Larry Bird led Boston to three more titles in the 1980s. Three times he was named league MVP. He also made 12 All-Star Games. Kevin McHale and Robert Parish were also stars on those teams.

The "Big 3" gave the Celtics their next title. It was in 2008. It consisted of Paul Pierce, Kevin Garnett, and Ray Allen. They beat the Lakers in the NBA Finals. Pierce played 15 years for the Celtics. He played in 10 All-Star Games.

## Other Celtics Stars

The Celtics have had many other stars. John Havlicek played 16 seasons with Boston. He made 13 All-Star Games. He was on eight Celtics title teams. Teammate Dave Cowens was an eight-time **all-star**.

Center Dave Cowens

Shooting guard Jaylen Brown

rnold "Red" Auerbach was a great coach. He later was an **executive**. He coached the Celtics for 16 years. He won nine titles. He won seven more titles as an executive.

Jayson Tatum and Jaylen Brown lead the Celtics today. They helped Boston win the title in 2024. Celtics fans hope they can help bring a record 19th title to Boston soon!

# About the Celtics

First season: 1946–47

Conference/division: Eastern Conference, Atlantic Division

Team colors: green, gold, and brown

Home arena: TD Garden

**NBA CHAMPIONSHIPS:**

1957, 4 games to 3 over St. Louis Hawks

1959, 4 games to 0 over Minneapolis Lakers

1960, 4 games to 3 over St. Louis Hawks

1961, 4 games to 1 over St. Louis Hawks

1962, 4 games to 3 over Los Angeles Lakers

1963, 4 games to 2 over Los Angeles Lakers

1964, 4 games to 1 over San Francisco Warriors

1965, 4 games to 1 over Los Angeles Lakers

1966, 4 games to 3 over Los Angeles Lakers

1968, 4 games to 2 over Los Angeles Lakers

1969, 4 games to 3 over Los Angeles Lakers

1974, 4 games to 3 over Milwaukee Bucks

1976, 4 games to 2 over Phoenix Suns

1981, 4 games to 2 over Houston Rockets

1984, 4 games to 3 over Los Angeles Lakers

1986, 4 games to 2 over Houston Rockets

2008, 4 games to 2 over Los Angeles Lakers

2024, 4 games to 1 over Dallas Mavericks

**TEAM WEBSITE:**

https://www.nba.com/celtics/

# Glossary

**all-star**—a player picked to play in the All-Star Game, featuring the season's top stars

**assist**—a basketball pass that leads to a basket

**barnstorming**—a tour that makes brief stops in many towns

**executive**—a person or group who has authority

**Most Valuable Player (MVP)**—an honor given to the season's best player

**rival**—a team that plays extra hard against another team

**title**—another word for championship

Power forward Kristaps Porziņģis

# Index